a stitch and
a prayer

phyllis tickle

a stitch and a prayer

a memoir of faith amidst war

PARACLETE PRESS
BREWSTER, MASSACHUSETTS

Library of Congress
Cataloging-in-Publication Data
Tickle, Phyllis.
A stitch and a prayer: a memoir of faith
amidst war/Phyllis Tickle.
    p. cm.
    ISBN 1-55725-340-4 (trade paper)
    1. Spiritual life—Christianity—Miscellanea.
2. World War, 1939-1945—Religious aspects—
Christianity—Miscellanea. 3. Tickle, Phyllis—
Childhood and youth—Miscellanea.
I. Title.

BV4501.3.T53 2003
277.3'0824'092— dc21
[B]   2003010941

10 9 8 7 6 5 4 3 2 1

©2003 by Phyllis Tickle

Original edition published in 1995
by The Upper Room, 1908 Grand Avenue,
Nashville, Tennessee 37202.

ISBN 1-55725-340-4

Published by Paraclete Press
Brewster, Massachusetts
www.paracletepress.com

Printed in the United States of America.

THIS BOOK IS
Dedicated to the memory of
Laura Simpson, a dark friend;

Was joyfully written for Snab,
whose book it always was;

Has been, from the beginning,
a gift for Dunlap and his cousins.

Books cannot be killed by fire. People die, but books never die. No man and no force can abolish memory. . . . In this war, we know, books are weapons.

Franklin Delano Roosevelt

Message to the American Booksellers Association

23 April 1942

PHILIP WADE ALEXANDER
was, to use the rhetoric of his century, a gentleman
and a scholar. Born in 1890 in rural, northwestern Tennessee
just below the bend where the mighty Mississippi
crooks at Missouri and meets the Ohio River, he went on to
become one of the mid-century's more prominent and
influential Southern educators. Neither his Huck Finn origins
nor his mature accomplishments were more than
tangentially interesting to me as a youngster, however. The
interesting, the absorbing, the vital thing was that he
was my father, and I was his only child. I absorbed him like a

budding branch absorbs the sun; and he was content to let me be what and as I would, under his benevolence.

There is a saying among writers—almost an axiom, in fact—which holds that every writer is possessed of only one story. Like a seductive echo, that story weaves back and forth, haunting, or else informing, everything its thrall ever attempts. As professional self-assessments go, this one is probably more accurate than most. Certainly it has proved itself accurate in my own particular case. It should come as no surprise, then, when I say that what follows here has been both the pervading bouquet and the leitmotif in everything I have ever fashioned during many years of plying the writer's craft.

When this little book was first published several years ago, it was presented as a remembrance. Now, in this time of

wars and rumors of war, it is being republished as a
memoir of another, earlier war. While *remembrance* is the
humbler and even dearer word, *memoir* is more fitting,
I suspect, for martial days. *Memoir* also acknowledges not
only my own presence in the story, but my role as its
constant architect as well. All of which is to say that what
you are about to read, while it is the story of my
father, is also the myth of my father. Each way of telling has
its own place in the relating of human affairs; yet ultimately
both are needed if one is to convey the whole truth . . .
and that axiom is never more germane than it is when one is
writing about a gentleman and a scholar.

Phyllis Tickle

The Farm In Lucy, Lent 1, 2003

a stitch and
a prayer

IT WAS THE WINTER OF 1937,
the deep dark winter of 1937, and I was almost
four. Still three, but almost four. Even I
knew that, in the all-engulfing, all incorporating   1
way of children when they deal with history or
time. And there was war in Europe. I knew that
too, but I knew it in a detached way.

War was a fact somewhere in my parents'
conversation. It was a circumstance wrapped so
snugly in the shades of their evening talk that I
could not make of it a familiar thing. I could not
even snatch a decent glimpse of it as it fled from
the probe of my questions. But it was there. That
is, it was there until it came to dinner one night.

There was an early twilight that evening. The
first hard freezes had already wilted and
burned away the last of my autumn pleasures and
confined me, rebellious and offended, to the
dim interiors of our campus apartment. Like all
mountain houses, ours too would be gray
and unmappable in its duskiness until a thick lay
of snow would come outside the windows,
bringing us its reflected light. But I had known
this sorrow before. I had learned to wait for
the snow and the winter's sharp, crisp light
flooding the playroom floor, and the cold joy
of my swing in the snowlight, and the blur of my
sled rushing down the hill behind the history

building, and the laughter of the undergraduates
as they snowballed each other and sometimes me,
and sometimes . . . although they always claimed it
as accidental . . . sometimes my professor father.

I knew these things, but I did not know about
phone calls yet, not phone calls at the dinner
hour in those lost years when the dinner hour was
eucharistic for those of us who gathered to it and
held inviolate even by those who did not.

My mother's pre-World War II phone was
of the newest design and one of the few vanities I
can ever remember her having invested in.
Mother's phone sat. In other words, it did not
hang, glued to an oak panel and bracketed

to the wall like most, nor did it require cranking in order to work. Black and pristine, her phone arose from its sleek round base with only half a body, or so it seemed to me. Only one arm hung from only one shoulder, but its mouth was beautiful, flared and trumpeting and almost always still warm from her conversations when I touched it.

When her phone rang that night at so unseemly and indecorous an hour, my mother waited, as was proper, for my father to excuse himself from the table to the living room and the whirring call.

I cannot remember now how he told her or how they told me or even if they did.

— — —

PERHAPS I GATHERED. THAT TOO IS
the way of children. By whatever means, however,
I came, before full nightfall, to understand
that war had taken on a new and more immediate
position in our lives. My uncle's ship had
been sunk at sea . . . torpedoed by the Germans
in the Atlantic trade routes just off the Azores.

I remember only my father's words, "He
shouldn't have tried it! I knew he should not have
tried it!" and my mother sitting at the table,
her chair pushed back from her place and the
picture frame from her dressing table clutched in

4–5

her left hand. I remember how white her hands
were and how her bracelet broke light across
the candlelit cloth. I remember that she did not
cry, only that she stared through the window
at the obscuring cold.

Young and lean, as dark of eyes and hair as she
herself was, my uncle, her youngest brother,
stared at me through her fingers. The chin below
his Porter nose cast a fine, patrician shadow
over the Merchant Marine uniform he was wearing.
As if to counterbalance the chin, he had set
the brim of his dress hat so that it too would cast
a shadow, a vague one, over his high left cheek.
I loved him.

It would be another ten years before I would
begin to use correctly words like *contraband cargo*
and *ammunitions* and *underground* and *resistance. Nazism*
and *Mein Kampf* and *Il Duce* were lost on one so
young and so secured; but not on the dashing
young uncle who sailed the Atlantic seaways for
his living and sent me postcards from half a
dozen ports. Nor were they lost on my parents
who had lived abroad for a year to two while my
father studied European instructional systems and
methodology. Such things were not lost on them.

In time, that marvelously healing capsule in
which we all are nurtured to a strength that will
sustain us outside of it. . . .

In time, the telephone would ring again, but it would be morning and I would be still half-wrapped in blanket dreams. I would hear my mother weep at last, the sound coming across the transom between my room and theirs; but her release would be dressed in my father's deeper laughter and I would understand in some unspoken way that the uncle had been rescued. Lacking any clear idea of the life of the sea, I would also lack any clear idea of what that meant. For years I would rather fancy the uncle as riding gaily into the port of Lisbon astride a Disney dolphin, his Porter chin still unscathed and the snap-brim dress hat still casting its shadow on his high left cheek.

After that, of course, war came closer.

We sat out the twilights of my fourth year in the living room by the new wireless. All over the world, dining room evenings with their fair linen and candles were fading away, and we were no exception.

— — —

APART FROM THE THRUMMING GLOW of the new radio's bulbous tubes, there was no light in the late afternoons where we sat as a family in my mother's parlor and listened to the sounds of a dying order. It was to me as if the parents were afraid somehow of those exquisite

lamps, afraid that their soft glow might chase
away the wireless's sound; might warm the corners
of the room and sap the intensity of their focus;
might add comfort where only despair was intense
enough to support us.

Eventually the Rock of Gibraltar's station was
the last free voice still coming out of Europe.
Clinging to that ancient Pillar of Hercules
like those lashed against the terrors of a roiling
sea, the outpost and those who broadcast
from it crackled for months across an ocean and
into our apartment before the winter afternoon
when they were no more. I watched as my
father, his fingers more tremulous with each spin

of his dials, adjusted and tuned and corrected,
all to no avail. Gibraltar was gone.

I saw my father cry for the first time that
afternoon. He sat in the shadowing room, his arms

crossed as if in self-embrace, and his tears
were crooked little streams down his stone-cast
face. He had fought in the First War, an expert in
cryptology and telegraphy. The loss of Gibraltar
meant another war. He was too old to go, too
young to watch. In the place of both, he wept.

The official declarations of war came shortly
thereafter, just as he had known they would, and
with them the hateful air-raid drills. Hours . . . or
so it seemed to me then . . . under the dining

room table, Mother's drapes sealed with ugly
paper tape hard against the window facings and
no light anywhere . . . hours when my father,
a block warden, patrolled unarmed and checking
. . . hours when the silence was an exquisite thirst
for any sound, but especially for that of the
all-clear and his key in the door again.

Within a year after that, the trips began. I did
not know why and I almost never knew where,
only that he was gone and that when he returned
his luggage was more filled with papers and taped-
shut folders than with his clothes and linen.
I remember that once, when he was unpacking, a
darling little lizard slithered frantically from

amongst his papers and across the bedroom floor.
I had never seen such a creature before and was as
enchanted as my mother was offended.

So soon as the creature and Mother's
consternation were both soothed, only my wonder
remained . . . my wonder and some vague
recognition that the suitcase had been to a distant
place far beyond the range of the flowers and
trees and creatures that I knew so personally and
so intricately.

Desert! It was a dangerous word. The lizard
frantic in my old fish bowl faded into all the
lizards in my *Child's Book of Wonder*. Desert. My
father had been to a place like the *Book of Wonder's*

12–13

desert. Willie (for I had named him almost immediately) died at some forgotten moment and departed this life unmourned. By the time of his death, even his exoticism had paled into nothingness compared to my father's.

— — —

THE YEARS DID PASS, AS EVEN YEARS of agony tend mercifully to do. Late phone calls and desert trips, air-raid drills and practiced blackouts, dark-hatted men at the front door and long hours behind other (and closed) doors . . . they all receded from our lives again. War was once more a monster appeased. Grumbling and

not yet sated, it was at least dormant enough so
that most of us who had been innocent in 1937
could grow up.

In time, that vessel whose walls are marked
and measured, graduated and imprinted by our
memory . . . in time, I would come upon some
consistency, some centralizing sanity, some motif
that, if it did not make sense of those years of
scarred childhood and of the ones that followed
it, did at least make some order out of them.
And I was to find that sanctuary in the memory of
my father's hands.

IN RETROSPECT I KNOW THAT THE education of my soul began sometime close to midnight on the night of that unnatural phone call with its messages of terror at sea. Sometime during the late evening hours lost to me now in no-recall, I had been put to bed. But if I cannot remember my going, I can vividly remember my rousing . . . the pounding in my breathways . . . the gasping cold of the floor beneath my bare feet . . . and the urgency which drove me to endure it in order to reach the safety of my parents' room.

The feral dark which had come to our dining room windows earlier and permitted my mother the comfort of its deceptive blankness was no

longer safely outside the windows. Sometime
during the hours I had slept, it had insinuated
itself like a miasma through the cracks in the cas-
ings and the draughts in the frames. It lay now, a
furred other-life, between me and the glow of
activity seeping in from around the closed door.

In my terror to shoot through the darkness
before it could realize and engulf me, I more
burst through than opened the door adjoining
the two bedrooms, yet neither of my parents
seemed to hear me. My mother lay, sleeping
at last, in her single bed. My father, still dressed
as at dinner, sat beside his larger, double one
with only his tie loosened. He had pulled

Mother's armless rocker, the one she called her sewing chair and which she always set by the window when she did her needlework, up close to the bed's edge. There he sat, hunched slightly forward over the bed's expanse with his massive shoulders curved slightly forward in concentration on something in front of him.

Mother's black, Chinese-lacquer workbasket was beside him on the bed, and at his feet was the tissue-lined box of yarn rosettes she had been weaving since late summer. Mesmerized by the incongruity of the delicate rosettes and the huge blunt fingers, I watched as my father lifted up yet another wool rosette from its place in the cardboard

box; set it tentatively at several different places
along the patchwork of rosettes he was making;
finally selected a place and began, crochet hook in
his hand, to secure the newcomer into the pattern
which lay, eight or nine rosettes long and in places
three or four rosettes deep, in front of him.

"Did Mama teach you to do that?" I blurted
the words, so great was my astonishment, but
he seemed not to hear them as an impertinence.
Indeed, if anything, he seemed more surprised by
my presence than distressed by my rudeness.

"No," he said, "My mama did, years ago," and
the hook flashed again.

"I never saw you do it before."

"More's the pity," he said. Then he added, more to himself than to me, "But perhaps I never needed it before."

"Does Mama know you're doing it?" Permission was hard to come by at our house. I was already old enough to know that all too well; and I could no more have prevented the question than I could have stopped the terrors of my night from embracing me.

"Yes."

He didn't look up from his work, but I could see the half-smile which always started, when he was amused, at the cleft beneath his nose and spread across his thin lips until it met again just

above the crevice of his chin. Thus emboldened, I
moved closer to him.

"And she doesn't care?" I was as much
impressed as amazed at this point.

"Yes, but she doesn't object."

I went back to bed, forgetful of whatever my
mission had been, of whatever demons had
beleaguered me, of whatever urgency had
threatened me. And even though the morning
brought my mother's tears of relief and my
father's healing laughter to rouse me, the events
of that pivotal evening were never destined to be
contained within it. Instead, they were to spread like
a secret mesh of vine and verdure across a lifetime.

The rosette coverlet—for that is what it was eventually to become—grew in my father's hands for all the years that stretched from the winter of 1937 to the horror of Hiroshima. Night after night, at evening's end, while the wireless tubes faded and cooled in the darkened living room, he would pour a glass of milk, make himself a plate of cheese and crackers, and move from the kitchen into the bedroom. There, drawing the armless rocker up beside his bed, he would sit and work.

Some nights he simply wove rosettes from the scraps and hanks of wool yarn which it was increasingly difficult for Mother and her friends to

locate and bring home to him. Some nights—ones,
I know now, when he felt some shaft of hope
piercing our mountain dark—he patterned the coverlet, assigning and then incorporating rosettes
he had already woven. As the War progressed,
Mother began to join him.

22–23

On the nights when they worked together, it
was Mother who sat in the rocker while he hooked
or wove, precariously perched on the edge of
his bed. Bed-setting was another prohibition that
was stringently enforced at our house, and
my father's obvious license to violate it amazed
more than a few of my childish evenings.
But even in those shared times of two parental

heads bent and two sets of parental hands busied, the rosettes were my father's work.

Although it was she who had begun the project, my mother never touched the coverlet again, except to admire it with him. She occupied herself instead with the ugly—or so I thought— khaki yarns that were issued to her every month by the Red Cross and from which she (and all the other women who knew how) were expected to knit heavy wool hosiery for Allied boots.

As the maw of war swallowed up year after colorless year, as the evenings of air drills and the days of rationing lines became, by their very repetitiousness, more and more burdensome, so

the pre-sleep hours in the bedroom seemed
too to increase, coming earlier and earlier into
our night's activities. Like monastics of any faith
who dream of surcease as they move to their
prayers, so my parents moved toward that
consoling space. There the salmon-tinted bulbs
of Mother's wall sconces suffused the last vestiges
of a lost decadence across the litany of their
hands, making benediction out of shadows
and familiarity. And there, before war's end, all
the metaphors of religion were to be brought
home to my young soul and given parental
permission to flourish within me.

24—25

— — —

FOR MONTHS WHILE IT WAS GROWING,
the rosette coverlet was stored each night, as
were all works in progress, in Mother's cedar
storage chest. As the War dragged on and the
coverlet grew, it became too bulky for the chest,
and my father was forced to leave it, large but
still unfinished, spread out on his bed.

By the spring of my eleventh year when
Normandy's beaches had been successfully
stormed and fear was a less ready guest, my mother
had taken to quipping that if the War did not
end soon, the coverlet would exceed even the
reaches of the bed. My father was obviously

pleased by her decreasing anxiety and smiled
that thin half-smile of his whenever she twitted
him; but he was not to be dissuaded. His weaving
and sewing no longer had anything to do either   26–27
with craft or with the coverlet. They had, instead,
become a discipline, and we all knew it.

Each stitch securing the petals of a rosette,
each thread woven to fill in a center, each loop
catching one into pattern . . . every individual
flash of needle or hook, in fact . . . had been
translated over the slow years into tangible prayer.
So long as he stitched, my father kept the faith
with those who could not—kept it until, as he so
biblically said, "this indignation be overpast."

By V-J Day, when he tied off his last stitch, the
rosettes had indeed grown to cover the bed
literally from the floor on one side to the floor
on the other side and from the floor at the
bed's foot to the edge of its head, back again to
cover the doubled pillows and then up, over, and
back around them. He had kept the faith.

My father never shaped another rosette after
that, and, so far as I know, he never picked up
another needle or held another thread again,
except as an incidental act born of a connoisseur's
affection. He contented himself instead with buying
huge quantities of stamped linen and fine
damasks for Mother, and elaborate canvasses for

petit point that she hated and he always wished her
to enjoy.

— — —

28–29

AS FOR HIS PART, MY FATHER TURNED,
at war's end, from needlecraft to wildflowers,
because there was at last gasoline enough to
allow him to roam our mountains in pursuit of
them; and to painting, because he admired
Mr. Churchill and because he found in the Prime
Minister's defense of the amateur painter a
rhetoric he wished to support. Yet the painting
he took up was not the Churchillian temerity
of colors splashed against a naked canvas. Rather,

my father began to tint by hand and with
incredible delicacy the photographs he had taught
himself to take with the new, post-War box cameras.

As with his wildflowers, by eliciting shadow and
light where none was, he created simple
beauties with no claim to any accolade beyond
joy, both his in the doing and the viewer's in
the seeing. In all those years of war, he said, he had
learned well the humility of the needle and of
those who build with it.

Midway of my childhood, we moved from our
campus quarters to ones of our own in town.
The new old house was selected, in no small part,
for the excellence of its secluded and sunny

gardens and for the brilliant lighting of its work-
room. There the quiet intensity of the old
rosettes became the illuminated intensity of the
new pointillized photographs, and the
perfumes of Mother's cedar chest became the
more fulsome ones of turned earth and
mountain loam. We had come full circle, back to
memory's earliest days, back to sunlit joys and
evening pleasures.

   But I who had learned by then to stitch and
knit and hook with skill, lacked my father's
gift with either oils or plants; I was forced to join
those restored hours of afternoon delights as
an observer rather than as an apprentice to his

30–31

wonders. It was a bitter time for me, and its longings still bite deeply into my appreciation of both his exquisite tints and his flower beds.

I asked him once (and only once) in the forgivable way of young adolescents, why he never stitched anymore. It was midsummer and we were in the shaded beds where he grew his trilliums and Solomon's seals. He didn't say anything at first, just trowelled on for a minute or two. When he did look up, there was a mist in his eyes, a gathering of memory in the corners, which I have never forgotten. He set his clump of plants down and studied me intently. I understood in that moment that he was gauging my years

and tallying carefully how far I might have come
in their brevity. "The coverlet is in me now," he
said. "I don't need to make another one. Can you
understand that?"

32–33

"Yes, sir." And in some numb, diffuse way it
was true. I did.

Reassured either by my answer or by its
surrogate of my earnestness, he returned to his
transplanting. "Besides," he said, his voice
directed more at the dark earth he had just
turned than at me, "I haven't stopped really. I'm
still stitching, just in other ways."

The July heat, normally moist and oppressive
in the mountains by that time of afternoon,

was transparent and warm around us like the affection of near kin. I can remember being conscious of the fact that even the apple trees had stopped leafing and chattering, and of the fact that I did not want to be distracted from my father's words by the abnormality of their silence.

"My mother was a piece of needlework," he said finally. His words had a kind of soft distance that made them more a logical sequel to his thoughts than a non sequitur in the conversation. "Maybe we all are in some ways. God knows we use enough of the language, don't we? . . . explaining ourselves to ourselves . . . 'hemming a fellow in' . . . 'knitting a family together' . . .

'spinning a yarn' . . . 'cutting the strings'. . . . " He
chuckled at his own chain of figures. "Metaphors,"
he said. "All metaphors, but what would we ever
do without them?"

34–35

He tamped dirt around the clump of lady
slippers he had just finished setting. "You're a lot
like my mother—loving with a needle the way
she was, but she always said that real needlework
took a tough spirit as well." He cut his eyes
up at me. I remember being chilled then, as if by
some fear of what he already knew and that
I had still to learn. "Being willing to decorate the
ordinary with the perishable requires courage, you
know . . . the same kind of courage as living does."

He sat back on his heels and reconsidered the
lady slippers. They were a constant frustration to
him, for they resisted to their own deaths his
repeated attempts to move them from their natal
elevations in the hills to our lower valley. Regardless
of how many sortees he made into the range which
encircled us and regardless of how many yards of
slippers he brought back with him, he could
never manage to sustain any profusion of them. I
was afraid for a minute that he would forget me
in his absorption with the recalcitrant transplants.
The apple trees and I waited together.

He stood up and brushed the grains of rotted
wood dirt off his pants legs. "I thought a lot about

my mother while I was working the coverlet. Did
you know that?"

This time I had no need to feign. I had indeed
known that. I nodded.

"She used to say that she could tell what a piece
of work had taught someone and who it was that
had been willing to learn." The thin smile spread
around the corners of his lips and rippled on
toward its center above his chin. "I wondered what
she would have said about the coverlet and me."

"Did it teach you anything?" Even though the
innocence of the wildflowers and the silence of the
apple trees had given me permission, his mood was
still broken, yanked back from reverie to reportage.

"Yes, of course, it did." He was impatient of his answer if not of my question. "All of those things you would suppose from a long, complicated project like that . . ."

Then his eyes drifted off of me again for just a moment and he said, "But mainly the coverlet showed me how it was—in what way it was, that is—that Mama was right. Stitches do take the time they are made in and spend it to change the people who are making them." His voice was hesitant and slightly higher than usual as if he were both tentative of his commentary and relieved to have found it. "Always remember that I told you that, Princess. Watch the people as much as their stitches." I always did.

When he died thirty-five years later, my father
was still sleeping under the rosette coverlet. I was
with him when he finally slipped away, and he
went calling for his mother. After the funeral,
Mother burned the rosette coverlet. It was the
only way she knew to send it to him and we could
not bear, either of us, to think of him without it.

38–39

All appearances to the contrary, this is not a book about   40–41
cottage handiwork and the domestic crafts, or at least it is
not a book about them as such. Nor is it a book about my
father really, though certainly it has been written in gratitude
to him.

No, instead this book is about a space interior to us all
and about how he taught me to go there . . . about that
space where what we think and what we do can sit a while
and be at peace with each other. This book is about
that place where the center holds, and the world external to
it is for a moment stilled.

When hands and thoughts are occupied in the goodness
of small and needful creation, the spirit rests that
deep rest in which it can attend itself and be attended by the
sacred. Distrustful always of the time and circumstance
entwined in human perceptions, my father spoke with his
attention the established prayers of the psalms and
the church and tradition; but he sent his spirit, refreshed and
whole, when he would speak as himself to God. The
result, like its motivation, was a singular reverence as well
as a simple gift that wanted passing along.

2003 A STITCH AND A PRAYER
A Memoir of Faith Amidst War by Phyllis Tickle.
Book design by Michele Wetherbee at doubleu-gee in
Petaluma, California. Typefaces are Mrs. Eaves designed by
Zuzana Licko, 1996; and Meta Plus designed by Erik
Spiekermann, 1991—1993. Cover photograph is of 2nd
Lt. Robert Edward English of Wellsboro, Pennsylvania,
b.1923—d.1944, maternal uncle of the designer.